TONY
BUZAN

SPEED
READING

Other Tony Buzan titles published by BBC Active:

Buzan Bites
Mind Mapping
Brilliant Memory

The Mind Set
Use Your Head
Use Your Memory
Master Your Memory
The Speed Reading Book
The Mind Map® Book
The Illustrated Mind Map® Book

Embracing Change

TONY BUZAN

SPEED READING

Educational Publishers LLP trading as BBC Active
Edinburgh Gate
Harlow
Essex CM20 2JE
England

First published in 2006 by BBC Active

ISBN: 0 563 5203 53

Commissioning Editor: Emma Shackleton
Project Editors: Sarah Sutton and Helena Caldon
Text Designer: Annette Peppis
Cover Designer: R&D&Co Design Ltd
Senior Production Controller: Man Fai Lau
Illustrator: Alan Burton
Printed in Spain at Mateu Cromo

The Publisher's policy is to use paper manufactured from sustainable forests.

CONTENTS

Introduction

⊙ Would you like to be able to read at a rate of 1000 words per minute?

⊙ Would you like to improve your concentration and comprehension?

⊙ Would you like to supercharge your ability to retain information?

⊙ Would you like to overcome learning difficulties, such as dyslexia?

⊙ Would you like to understand how your eyes and brain connect to absorb and retain information?

⊙ Would you like to increase your vocabulary and general comprehension?

If you have answered a resounding 'yes' to these questions, I am pleased to tell you that you will be able to achieve all these goals and more once you have been introduced to my Mental Literacy techniques. Learning to speed read easily and without effort is considered by many to be one of life's most rewarding and significant achievements. It is a skill that, with some patience and practice, is at everyone's fingertips.

We are at a period in our evolution where information is cheap; it is easily available via the Internet, email, myriad newspapers, reports, journals, letters and other sources. The skill of Speed Reading will revolutionize your ability to prioritize and retain essential information.

The main purposes in learning to Speed Read successfully are:

⊙ To increase your reading speeds dramatically.

⊙ To improve your levels of concentration and comprehension.

⊙ To increase your understanding of how your eyes and brain work.

⊙ To improve your vocabulary and general knowledge.

⊙ To save you time and build your confidence.

The problems to overcome are:

⊙ Deciding what to read: the art of selection.

⊙ Understanding what you read: effective note-taking and comprehension.

⊙ Retaining information: how to remember what you want to know.

⊙ Recalling information: having the ability to recall, on demand, the facts you want and having them at your fingertips.

Drawing on the techniques explained in more depth in my books *Use Your Head* and *The Speed Reading Book*, I have created this bite-sized book for time-starved people on the move who want to learn to speed read, so that they can take in more of the information that the world has to offer. The techniques will give you an advantage in every area of your life and free up precious time to enjoy other aspects. You need never miss an important engagement because of a reading assignment again.

Throughout this book I will give you easily digestible pieces of information to help you to understand, improve and enhance your ability to read and retain information. You will learn practical techniques and exercises that will work *with* your brain so that your brain works more effectively and more efficiently than ever before.

My interest in speed reading has its roots in childhood. When I was 14 years old my classmates and I were given a series of aptitude tests to perform. I was thrilled to discover that I had a reading speed of 213 words per minute – until my teacher told me that that was an average score. The person in the class with the highest score had achieved 314 wpm. The teacher then dealt a real blow when he announced that there was nothing one could do to improve one's ability to read faster. He believed it was a skill one was born with and could not change.

This made no sense to me as I had achieved considerable improvements in my physical fitness through exercise. Surely, I thought, it must be possible to develop mental and visual exercises that would improve my brain's capacity to learn, as well as enhance my ability to speed read and comprehend information?

These questions took me on a search that continues to this day. Soon after my life-changing test, I was passing the reading barrier at 400 wpm; eventually moving up to 1000 wpm. The lesson for me was that:

Reading is to the mind what aerobic exercise is to the body.

My fascination with how the brain works developed into a lifetime's passion. This book contains a distillation of the mental literacy techniques that I have developed during my years of working in this field. Whether you are 7, 17, 77 or 107 years old, you will find benefit in these techniques – and I hope you find them as exciting as I have done.

Enjoy your speed reading journey!

Tony Buzan

'Tony Buzan's clearly explained step-by-step system…is like the opening of a door into a world thick with the golden sunshine of knowledge.'

The Late Heinz Norden, former Editor,
The Encyclopedia of Knowledge

1 SPEED READING AND YOUR BRAIN

This book has several core aims:
- To improve your reading speed dramatically.
- To improve and maintain your comprehension.
- To increase your understanding of the function of your eyes and brain and to be able to use them more effectively.
- To help you to read and study more efficiently, and to bring speed reading into every aspect of your life.
- To help you improve your vocabulary and general knowledge.
- To save you time.
- To increase your confidence.

Those are quite large claims from such a bite-sized volume!

However, the techniques that you will learn in order to achieve these aims include:
- Self-assessment: How fast do you read?
- Guided reading techniques that will help you to take in more information more quickly from the written page.
- Tips on how to turn common reading problems to your advantage.
- Guidance on how to concentrate better, understand more, scan and skim information to get to the crux of the matter, and how to create your environment to work with you.

Once you have learned the basics, we will up the pace with a section that includes guidance on how to increase your vocabulary to include new prefixes, suffices and word roots. This has the potential to increase your vocabulary from 1000 words to 10,000 words with very little effort.

The speed reading systems described in this book are designed to work with your brain; to stimulate your senses and to help your memory to store the information you choose to feed it in an ordered and easily accessible fashion.

In the pages that follow I will give you a new definition of reading and introduce you to all the key skills involved in speed reading – which is a complete process of knowledge assimilation. Individual chapters will explain how you read; how speed reading works; how you can overcome reading problems; how to increase your perception, improve your concentration and mastermind your vocabulary.

Watch your speed

There are many advantages for your brain in learning to speed read:

◉ Your eyes will work less hard physically, because you will not need to pause as often to absorb the information you are reading.

◉ The rhythm and flow of the speed reading process will allow you to absorb the meaning of what you are reading with greater ease. (A slower reading pace encourages more scope for pauses, boredom and loss of concentration, which inhibits comprehension and slows understanding.)

If you would like to monitor your speed reading progress as you practise, use the following steps and register your progress on the progress chart featured on page 87 of this book.

It may be helpful to select a book now that you will use specifically for assessing your speed-reading progress. In that way, as you move through the chapters you will get a true picture of the progress you are making, day by day and week by week.

I can promise you that if you follow the techniques in this book you will see a marked improvement when you re-visit the test later on. The more you practise, the faster and more effective your speed reading ability will become, so use the chart as frequently as you like; whether once a day, once a week, or once every month or so.

Why not test your current reading speed right now, before you start following my techniques?

To calculate your speed in words per minute, take the following steps:

1 Read for one minute – note your start and stopping points within the text.

2 Count the number of words on three lines.

3 Divide that number by three to give you the average number of words per line.

4 Count the number of lines read (balancing short lines out).

5 Multiply the average number of words per line by the number of lines you read; this will give you your reading speed in words per minute (wpm).

Expressed as an equation, the formula for working out speed in wpm is:

$$\text{wpm (speed)} = \frac{\text{number of pages read} \times \text{number of words per average page}}{\text{number of minutes spent reading}}$$

If you work with your brain in the ways described, you can't help but learn to speed read, which will add immense value to your experience of learning and understanding as a result.

2 HOW YOU READ

Reviewing beliefs about reading

Have you ever stopped to think about how you read and assimilate information? Before starting to learn speed reading techniques that will allow you to read as many as 1000 words per minute, take a moment to answer the following questions. Would you reply 'True' or 'False' to the following statements?

⊙ Words are read one at a time.

⊙ Reading faster than 500 words per minute is impossible.

⊙ If you read fast you are not able to appreciate what you are reading.

⊙ High reading speeds mean lower levels of concentration.

⊙ Average reading speeds are natural, and therefore the best way to learn.

The answer to all five questions is 'False'. Let me explain why:

⊙ Words are read one at a time.

False – *We read for meaning, not for single words.*

⊙ Reading faster than 500 words per minute is impossible.

False – *We have the capacity to take in as many as six words at a time and as many as twenty-four words a second.*

⊙ If you read fast you are not able to appreciate what you are reading.

False – *The faster reader will understand more of what is being expressed, will experience greater levels of concentration and will have time to review areas of special interest and relevance.*

⊙ High reading speeds mean lower levels of concentration.

False – *The faster we read, the more impetus we gather and the more we concentrate.*

⊙ Average reading speeds are natural, and therefore the best way to learn.

False – *Average reading speeds are* not *natural; they are simply the result of the limitations of the way we were taught to read.*

Changing a personal belief about what is possible will help you to understand the process of speed reading; it will also encourage your success because your mind will not be hindering your progress with the weight of false assumptions.

Eye movements

If I were to sit with you as you read this book and ask you to show me with your forefinger how you believe your eye moves across the page, what do you think the speed and path of that movement would look like? The majority of people would trace each line of text in straight lines from left to right, as they move gradually down the page.

The path of movement would look something like this:

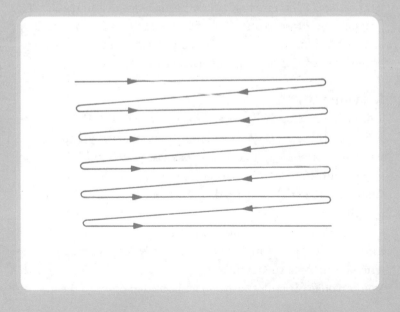

When children learn to read they often follow the line of the words across the page with a forefinger to help concentration and direction. Traditionally they are discouraged from doing this, as there is a mistaken belief that the technique will slow them down. We now know that it is not the movement or direction of their finger that slows down their reading process, but the speed at which they move their finger. So instead of asking them to stop doing this, we should be encouraging children to move their finger across the page faster! (See Chapter 4 for more information about the reasons for this.)

In practice, a thin visual aid such as a pencil or a pen is preferable to a finger, as there will be less chance of the guide obliterating some of the words.

Speed

The average reader takes in approximately 200–240 words per minutes. When we read, our eyes make small and regular 'jumps', pausing or 'fixating' in order to take in information. It is possible to make an immediate improvement in your reading speed by spending less time on each pause.

Movement

Taking in text line by line *is* an effective way to absorb information, but it is not the fastest. There are many different pathways for our eyes to travel across a page and still successfully absorb information – as I will explain in detail in Chapter 5. (See the pathway diagrams on pages 40–1.)

The eye does not move smoothly in one continuous sweep across the page; it stops and starts in order to take in information. Interestingly, the eye can only see things *clearly* when it can 'hold them still':

◉ If an object is still, the eye must be still in order to see it.

◉ If an object is moving, the eye must move with the object in order to see it.

Test this for yourself by holding a finger in front of your eyes. When it is still, your eyes are still; when it moves, your eyes follow it in order to see it. In relation to reading, this means that the eye has to *pause* to take in the words, *because the words are static*.

This is a critical speed reading concept.

When your eyes pause, they can take in up to five or six words at a time so they can easily fixate after the beginning and before the end of the line, thus taking in the information 'to the side'. If you use a visual aid, it will minimize the amount of work that your eyes have to do, keeps the brain focused and maintains constant reading speeds, combined with high levels of understanding.

The following three figures on page 20 show:
(A) The basic 'stop and start' movement of your eye during reading.
(B) The poor reading habits of a slow or unfocused reader.
(C) The eye movements of a more efficient reader.

Figure (B) shows what happens in the eye movements of a poor reader. This reader pauses or fixates on words for twice as long as most people. Extra pauses are caused because the reader often re-reads words, sometimes skipping back in as many as three places to make sure that the correct meaning has been taken in. Research has shown that, in 80 per cent of cases when readers were not allowed to skip back or regress, they *had* taken in all the necessary information.

Figure (C) shows that the good reader, while not back-skipping or regressing, also has longer jumps between groups of words.

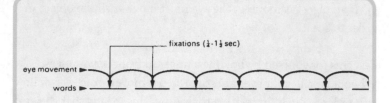

Figure A: Diagram representing the stop-and-start movement or 'jumps' of the eyes during the reading process.

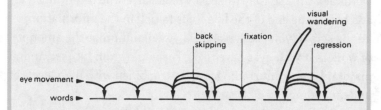

Figure B: Diagram showing poor reading habits of a slow reader: one word read at a time, with unconscious back-skipping, visual wanderings and conscious regressions.

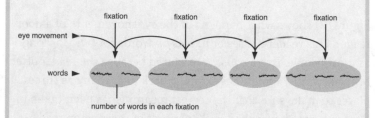

Figure C: Diagram showing eye movements of a better and more efficient reader. More words are taken in at each fixation, and back-skipping, regression and visual wandering are reduced.

On a normal page of 12 words per line, the weaker reader will fixate on single words, back-skip and regress while reading, pausing approximately 14 times, for an average of ½ a second per pause. That's a delay of 7 seconds per line. A speed reader, on the other hand, with minor adjustments and no interruptions would delay no more than two seconds per line.

The techniques in the following chapters are designed to overcome the common problems of back-skipping, visual wandering and regression that impede progress and will instead lead you towards taking in more and more words each time your eyes fixate on the page, as in (C).

An increase in reading speed leads to an automatic increase in comprehension. This is because the information is organized into meaningful chunks that make immediate sense to your brain.

3 SEVEN STEPS TO SPEED UP YOUR READING

What is speed reading?

It will be helpful when learning to speed read to have a clear understanding of what we mean by 'reading' and what it involves, so that you are consciously involved in the process and understand your brain's involvement, too. Reading is usually described as 'getting from a book what the author intended' or, 'assimilating the written word', but I believe it should be defined as:

> **Reading is the individual's total interrelationship with symbolic information.**

I mean by this that reading is a process that is taking place on many different levels at the same time – and it is usually related to the *visual* aspect of learning, i.e., what we can see. For reading to be informative and for reading methods to be effective, the following seven levels of understanding need to be included. Every level must be further developed if you are to become an effective speed reader.

1 Recognition
2 Assimilation
3 Comprehension
4 Knowledge
5 Retention
6 Recall
7 Communication

Recognition

Definition: The reader's knowledge of the alphabetic symbols. This step takes place before the physical aspect of reading begins.

Assimilation
Definition: The physical process by which light is reflected from the word and is received by the eye. It is then transmitted via the optic nerve to the brain.

Comprehension
Definition: The linking together of all parts of the information being read with all other appropriate information. This includes words, figures, concepts, facts, pictures, etc. (I call this 'intra-integration'.)

Knowledge
Definition: The process by which the reader brings the whole body of his previous knowledge to the new information that he is reading, whilst making the appropriate connections. This includes analysis, criticism, appreciation, selection and rejection of information. (I call this 'extra-integration'.)

Retention
Definition: The basic storage of information. Storage can itself become a problem; most readers will have experienced the anxiety of being in an examination and having trouble retrieving some of that essential information successfully! Storage on its own is not enough – it must be accompanied by 'recall'.

Recall
Definition: The ability to retrieve from storage the information that is needed, ideally *when* it is needed.

Communication
Definition: The use to which the acquired information is immediately or eventually put, including written and spoken

communication, as well as dance, art and other forms of artistic expression. Importantly, communication also includes that all-important function – thinking.

All of the reading problems listed on page 7 of the introduction can be overcome by addressing one or more of these levels of understanding. Other influences, such as your surroundings, the time of day, energy levels, motivation, wellness and level of interest, are taken into account in Chapter 6.

4 BEAT READING 'PROBLEMS'

Why reading problems exist

Many of us hold false beliefs about reading and our ability to read. Take a moment to think about what you consider to be your problems with reading.

The issues most commonly experienced are listed below:

Vision   Speed   Comprehension   Time
Amount   Noting   Retention   Fear
Fatigue   Boredom   Analysis   Organization
Regression   Recall   Vocabulary
Subvocalization   Selection   Rejection
Concentration   Back-skipping

These traits are not the result of lack of ability, but of negative self-belief, inappropriate teaching methods, or a lack of understanding about how the eyes and brain work together to assimilate information.

When you learned to read you probably did so with either the 'phonic' (also known as Alphabet method), or the Look and Say method. In simple terms, the phonic method first teaches the child the alphabet, followed by the sounds of each of the letters, then the blending of these sounds into syllables, and finally the further blending of these sounds to form words. The Look and Say method teaches children to read by presenting them with cards, on which there are pictures. The names of the objects are clearly shown underneath the images. Once the child is familiar with both the image and the word, the images are removed, leaving only the words.

These methods are adequate for teaching children to learn words, but they are inadequate to encourage them to learn the *complete* process of taking in, assimilating and retaining information that uses the whole of the brain, not just the eyes.

'Once a problem is faced, analyzed and understood it becomes a positive energy centre for the creation of solutions.'

Common traits associated with so-called reading 'problems' are sub-vocalization (the practice of moving your lips while reading), finger-pointing, regression and back-skipping. Not all of these are problems in the true sense, and with a change of perspective are positively beneficial. This section looks at strategies for managing each of these traits, and illustrates some benefits.

Sub-vocalization

The tendency to 'mouth' words as you are reading is known as sub-vocalization. It is a natural stage in learning to read and is common in children who are taught to read out loud using the phonic method (see page 28). Sub-vocalization can be a barrier to learning to speed read for some people if they are dependent upon it for understanding, because it may slow down the rate at which words are read. However, it is quite possible for your brain to sub-vocalize 2000 words per minute – so there is no problem at all!

The advantage of sub-vocalization is that it can reinforce what is being read. You can choose to use the inner voice selectively – to emphasize important words or concepts – by increasing the volume on demand and literally shouting them out internally! The technique then becomes a positive memory aid.

Sub-vocalization can be of positive benefit to dyslexic readers, because internalizing the sound of the words as they are read will provide a reminder of the shape of the individual letters and will appeal to both the right and left sides of the brain.

Finger-pointing

To understand the difference between aided and unaided eye movement, try this experiment with a friend: one partner imagines a large circle . They then follow the outline exactly with their eyes. Almost without exception, this first exersize produces a shape which is very far removed from a circle! It is more like a battered line in the figure on the left below, and most people find the exercize difficult.

Now repeat the process, but the second partner asks the first partner to follow thier finger as they trace the shape of a circle in the air. Most people find that the eyes will move swiftly and almost perfectly in a circular direction.

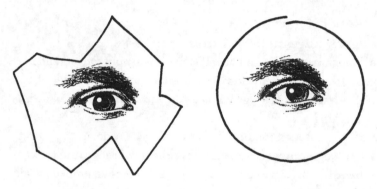

Pattern showing unaided eye movement attempting to move around the circumference of a circle.

Pattern showing aided eye movement around the circumference of a circle.

Most people who try this experiment will find that they are more comfortable having a guide to follow, which makes their eyes far more relaxed and efficient. This is because the eyes are designed to follow movement. Spotting movement is an instinctive function that was linked originally with survival, but continues to be vital to seeing and understanding what is going on in your environment.

Far from being a disadvantage, finger-pointing can actually help in learning to speed read. I would simply recommend that you may prefer to use a slimmer, purpose-designed reading aid, since fingers can be large and bulky and may obscure some words.

> ◉ There is a range of guided-reading techniques described in Chapter 5 that are essential tools for all masters of speed reading.

Regression and back-skipping

Although regression and back-skipping are slightly different traits, they both are related to a lack of confidence and a tendency to stay in a reading 'comfort zone'.

> ◉ Regression is the conscious process of returning to words, phrases or paragraphs that you feel you must have missed or misunderstood.
> ◉ Back-skipping is a similar but unconscious process of re-reading material that has just been read.

Re-reading material has been shown to make no difference to levels of understanding, so all you are doing is putting added pressure on your eyes. The simplest way to force yourself to break these habits is to increase your reading speed, and to maintain a rhythm as you read.

In conclusion, my experience over several decades of working with people who have been diagnosed with reading 'problems' is that many people do not have a problem at all. As we have seen, sub-vocalization and finger-pointing are not problems at all, while back-skipping and regressing are simply habits that can be altered.

5   YOUR AMAZING EYES

Each of your eyes is an amazing optical instrument, far superior in its precision and complexity to the most advanced telescope or microscope. We have known for some time that our pupils adjust their size according to the intensity of light and the nearness of the object viewed. The brighter the light and the nearer the object, the smaller the size of the pupil.

We also know that pupil size adjusts in tune with emotion, so if, for example, you are gazing at someone you are attracted to, your pupil size will increase automatically.

> ⊙ **As a speed reader, if you are interested in the subject you are reading about your pupils will dilate, letting in more light. This enables your brain, with no additional effort, to take in more data per second.**

How do your eyes 'read' information?

The retina at the back of the eye is a light receiver. When your eye takes in a range of complex images, the retinal light receivers decode the images and send them along the optic nerve to the visual area of the brain, known as the occipital lobe.

The occipital lobe is located not behind the eyes, but at the back of your head; so the popular phrase is correct; we really do have eyes 'in the back of the head'!

It is this occipital lobe that does your reading and directs your eyes around the page to hunt for information that is of interest. This knowledge forms the basis of the revolutionary approach to speed reading that is explained in this book.

Increase your perception AND expand your visual power

As you know from reading pages 19–20, your eyes are able to take in several words at a glance when they are reading from line to line. The next series of exercises is designed to expand your visual power so that you are able to take in more words 'at a glance' when you look at a page.

Measuring your horizontal and vertical vision

Read through these instructions once first before trying the technique or, alternatively, ask someone to read the passage to you while you follow the directions:

Look straight ahead and focus your attention on a point on the horizon as far away as possible, then:

⊙ Touch the tips of your two forefingers together so that they form a *horizontal* line, then hold them approximately 10cm in front of your nose.

⊙ While keeping your eyes fixed on your chosen point in the distance, begin to wiggle the tips of your fingers and move them apart slowly, along a straight, horizontal line. (You will need to move your arms and elbows apart as well, but keep the movement horizontal.)

⊙ Keep going until your fingers move just outside your field of vision and you can no longer see the movement of your fingers out of the corner of your eyes.

⊙ Stop and measure how far apart your fingers are.

Now repeat the exercise, but with one forefinger pointing upwards and the other downwards, so that the fingertips meet in a *vertical* line this time. Again, hold them together, approximately 10cm in front of your nose.

⊙ While keeping your eyes fixed firmly on your chosen point in the distance, begin to wiggle your fingers and move them apart – one upwards, one downwards – in a vertical line so that they gradually move out of the top and bottom of your field of vision.
⊙ Stop and measure how far apart your fingers are.

Does it surprise you to find out just how much and how far you can see when you are apparently focused solely on something else? How is this possible?

The answer lies in the unique design of the human eye. Each of your eyes has 130 million light receivers in its retina, which means that you have 260 million receivers of light in total. Your central focus (that part which you use to read your book, or focus on the point in the distance) takes up only 20 per cent of this light receiving capacity. The rest – that is 80 per cent of the total light receivers – are devoted to your peripheral vision.

By learning to make greater use of your peripheral vision while you are reading, you will begin to utilize the vast untapped potential of your peripheral vision: *your mind's eye.* What do I mean by the 'mind's eye'? I mean the ability to read or see with your entire brain, not just with your eyes. It is a concept that is recognized by those who practise yoga, meditation, prayer and anyone familiar with learning to 'see' *Magic Eye*™ three-dimensional pictures.

See with your mind's eye

When you have read through the guidelines of the following exercise, turn to page 39 and place your finger directly underneath the word 'fraction' in the middle of the page. Keeping your eyes totally focused on that central word, and without moving them:

⊙ See how many words you can observe to either side of the central word.

⊙ See how many words you can make out clearly above and below the word you are pointing at.

⊙ See if you can tell whether there is a number at the top or the bottom of the page, and if so, what that number is.

⊙ See whether you can count the number of paragraphs on the page.

⊙ See whether you can count the number of paragraphs on the opposite page.

⊙ Can you see a diagram on either of the pages?

⊙ If there is a diagram, can you determine clearly or roughly what it is illustrating?

Most people answer 'yes' to the majority of these questions, which shows that most people have the innate capacity to read using their peripheral vision as well as their central vision. By this means, you use all 260 million of your eye's light receivers to communicate with and illuminate your brain.

This revolutionary new approach means that from now on, you will read with your brain and not just with your eyes. The image on page 38 shows clearly the two levels of vision that are available. The inner circle of vision is the one that we are all familiar with; the outer circle shows the field of peripheral vision that is available to us, if we choose to use it.

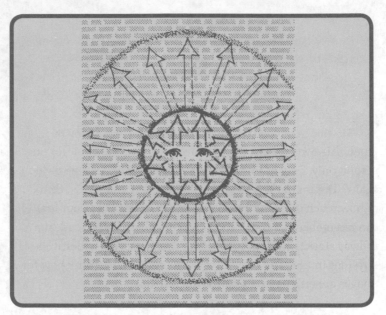

Fields of vision. The inner circled area shows the area of clear vision available to the speed reader when the eye/brain system is used properly. The outer circle shows the peripheral vision also available.

Reading bites

⊙ If you are able to combine peripheral vision with central focus you will be able to see and absorb information from entire paragraphs and pages at the same time.

⊙ You can expand your peripheral vision by holding your book further away from your eyes than usual. It will enable your peripheral vision to work better.

⊙ While your central focus is taking in the detail line by line, your peripheral vision is able to review what has been read and assess the value of what is to come.

⊙ This practice is also easier on the eyes, as they do not need to over-work their muscles.

Remember: it is your brain that reads – your eyes are just the very sophisticated lenses that it uses to do so.

Nine ways to super-power your vision

Open this book (or any book) at any page, and look at it for one second only. Do you think you could recognize the same page again? The answer is 'yes'. If you doubt the truth of this, think of how much information your eyes can take in and your brain can remember in a fraction of a second when on the road, at a railway station, or anywhere where you are seeing a multitude of different images and influences at the same time. Think how few images are on a page of text in comparison.

We each have the capacity to have a photographic memory: the key is to learn how to see.

Guided reading techniques

The nine reading techniques that follow are super-powered variations of the simple guided reading example in Chapter 4. It is useful to first practise each technique at very high reading speed – without pausing or worrying about whether or not you understand what you are reading.

The next step is to practise each technique at normal speed. In this way your brain will gradually become accustomed to your faster reading speeds. (You may find it useful to begin by re-reading familiar material. In this way you have the benefit of reviewing something that you already know, while 'warming up' your brain for the tasks ahead.)

The double-line sweep

The double-line sweep is very similar to the line by line approach illustrated on page 17. The difference is that your eye is encouraged to take in two lines of text at a time. It is a technique that combines both vertical and horizontal vision.

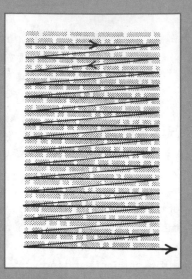

If you are a musician, you will probably find that you take to this technique with ease, as it is the same skill you apply when reading music.

The variable sweep

The variable sweep takes the same approach as the single- and double-line sweep, but allows you to take in the number of lines that you can cope with at one time.

The reverse sweep

This technique is identical to those above but with one significant difference: you are altering the process to review each section of text in reverse. This may sound absurd, but it makes sense if you recall that the eye can only take in information by fixing attention, and that words are viewed in groups of five or six.

In reading backwards you are simply 'holding' all the information you have in your mind, until you receive the final piece of the jigsaw at the start of each line. This has the benefit of enabling you to review the text at the same time as reading it – which will speed up your reading and improve your levels of concentration and comprehension.

Each of these 'sweep' techniques can be used for previewing, skimming or scanning for information, and you can take in as many lines as you choose. You can shorten (by taking in fewer lines) or lengthen (by taking in more lines) your sweeps, or combine more than one technique.

As you practise, your reading speed and comprehension will develop rapidly. Once you are comfortable using these techniques you may like to try more advanced variations described in full in *The Speed Reading Book* (BBC Active).

You can practise by reading any book on your shelves, but if you would like to measure how you have progressed in skill since you first embarked on your speed reading programme, please turn to page 75 and re-visit the 'Self Test'.

6 SUPERCHARGE YOUR SPEED READING

This chapter will explore and improve your speed reading skills, particularly:

⊙ Your powers of concentration.

⊙ Your ability to skim and scan information.

⊙ How your environment influences your ability to learn.

Improving concentration

In my experience of teaching and lecturing around the world I have found that 99.9 per cent of people believe that they suffer from periods of poor concentration. Many people say that they find themselves daydreaming instead of applying themselves to the task in hand. In fact, this is good news and is perfectly natural. Daydreaming occurs naturally every 30–40 minutes and it is your brain's way of taking a break in order to absorb what it has learnt.

If you think about it, you have not actually lost concentration, you have just chosen to concentrate on a series of other points of interest instead: the cat on the chair; the telephone ringing; a piece of music on the radio; or someone walking along the street – to name but a few distractions.

The problem is not your powers of concentration, but the direction and focus of that concentration.

When you master the art of concentration your entire eye/brain system becomes laser-like, with an extraordinary ability to focus and absorb information. The next section looks at some common enemies of concentration and suggests some methods that will help you get yourself back in focus:

The causes of poor concentration

Vocabulary difficulties

Efficient and concentrated speed reading relies upon a smooth flow of information with few interruptions in understanding. Pauses to look up words or to ponder will break your concentration and slow your understanding of the whole. If you come across a word that you don't understand when reading, rather than looking it up straight away, underline it and review it afterwards. (Information on vocabulary analysis in the next chapter is designed to help you to master your vocabulary and learn how to 'decode' unfamiliar words.)

Conceptual difficulties

If you don't really understand the concepts you are reading about you will have difficulty to concentrating. To get past this obstacle, choose one of the guiding techniques outlined on pages 40–1 and use skimming and scanning as ways of multiple-reading the material until it becomes familiar to you.

Inappropriate reading speed

Many people believe (because that is what they were taught) that reading things slowly and carefully will help understanding and comprehension. This approach is actually counter-productive and far from aiding your brain, reading slowly will actually slow it down. To check this out, try reading the following statement exactly as it is laid out. Read it 'slowly and carefully':

Speed read ing has be en found to be bet ter for under stand ing than slow read ing.

You probably found that hard work because your brain is not designed to take in information at such a slow pace. If you skim read it fast, the words will make instant sense.

Reading slowly and carefully encourages your brain to read more and more slowly, with less and less comprehension.

Now read the following sentence, this time reading the words as they are grouped:

**It has been discovered   that the human brain
with the help   of its eyes   takes in information
far more easily   when   the information
is conveniently grouped   in meaningful   bundles.**

An increase in the speed of reading leads to an automatic increase in comprehension. If you apply the speed reading techniques outlined in this book your brain will develop the capacity to organize words into meaningful groups as you read. By learning to adjust the speed and range of your reading you will have control and choice over the appropriate speed for the task in hand.

Poor concentration
Another common enemy of concentration is allowing your mind to remain focused on something else, instead of the task in hand. For example, you may need to finish reading an important report for a meeting early tomorrow morning, but your mind keeps wandering to your kids, to the disagreement you had with your business partner, to money worries, to which restaurant you should book for dinner tomorrow.

If you find yourself getting easily distracted from the task in hand, you will need to 'shake off' the threads of thought that are diverting you by refocusing on what you are trying to achieve. You may even want to stop for a moment to write down (or Mind Map) your current aims in order to gather your thoughts.

Poor organization

Poor organization is a common problem and sitting down to read something can sometimes feel like a personal battle. Having begun to read, the distractions begin: you have no pencil, cup of coffee, notepaper, spectacles, and so on. Constant distractions make it harder to build the impetus to begin again. The answer is simple: plan ahead so that you have everything you need close to hand, set yourself achievement targets and plan your breaks to coincide with completion of those tasks.

Lack of interest

An apparent lack of interest is often linked to other difficulties. For example: confusing material, lack of specialist vocabulary, conflicting priorities, negative attitude and other obstacles to concentration that are listed above. It is worth trying to solve these related issues first and then, if necessary, apply the 'harsh critic' approach.

Get annoyed with the material you are trying to read. In that way you will be drawn in, in the way you would to a debate with someone whose opinions you oppose.

Lack of motivation

Lack of motivation relates to a lack of goal. If you don't know why you are reading something it can be hard to motivate yourself to be interested in reading it.

Review your goals. It's an obvious thing to say, but once you become clear about why you need to absorb the information you will be better able to complete the task. Look back at the other points listed on pages 46–7. Use organization and personal interest to realign yourself with your target, and use your preferred guided reading technique to ensure that you complete the task as quickly as possible – and with optimum return. Of course, if your goal is no longer important to you, then you can choose to read something else!

Thomas Jefferson was president of the United States of America from 1801–9. He was renowned for his intellect and his capacity to speed read. The secret of his success lies in the advice he gave to others: you should know

'where you are, and what you are doing, and what time it is, and whether you are falling short of your schedule or not, and if so, how far short.'

The point he was making is that focus and planning are the keys to success. If those are in place, and you are committed to achieving your goal, you have no choice but to remain focused and to concentrate fully.

Scanning and skimming

Scanning and skimming are designed to combine your recently acquired skill of guided reading with special emphasis on *mental set*: the way your brain can pre-select information automatically.

> **O Scanning and skimming are used by the majority of speed readers.**
> **O Scanning and skimming can be enhanced when used together with a guided reading technique (see Chapter 5).**

Scanning

Scanning is a natural skill. You use it when you are scanning a crowd for a face that you know, or when you are scanning a road sign for relevant directions. We use scanning when the eye glances over a range of material to find a very specific piece of information. It is a simpler process than skimming (explained below) and is usually used in the context of text when you need to look something up: a name in a telephone directory, a particular piece of information in a book or a report, or a relevant link on a website.

As long as you know what you are looking for in advance and understand how the information is organized (for example, in alphabetical order or by theme), then this technique is simple.

> **Scanning is a process that is used to find *particular information*.**

Skimming

Skimming is a more complex method than scanning and is similar to the guided reading skill explained in Chapter 5. It is used to gain a general overview of information so that the 'bricks and mortar' of the content are understood.

Efficient skim reading can be done at speeds of approximately 1000 words per minute, while still gaining an outline understanding of what is being said.

> **Skimming is a process that is used to acquire a general overview of material.**

Are you sitting comfortably ...?

Your environment will affect your level of achievement, and your sense of physical well being will influence your ability to take in information. If you are feeling negative or unwell, your state of being will have a negative influence on your productivity. If, on the other hand, you are happy in your environment and inwardly content, you will react positively to reading and comprehend new information. It therefore makes sense to ensure that your environment is as uplifting and positive as possible.

Placement and intensity of light

Whenever possible, it is best to read or study in natural daylight, so your desk or reading platform should ideally be placed near a window. At other times, artificial light should come over your shoulder, opposite the hand with which you write. The lamp should be bright enough to illuminate the material being read, but not so bright that it provides a contrast with the rest of the room.

Availability of materials

To enable your brain to work comfortably and in a focused way, it is useful to have all the work materials and reference guides that you might need placed easily to hand. It will help you feel prepared and relaxed and better able to concentrate on the task.

Physical comfort

Making yourself too comfortable is counter-productive, because you will be tempted to fall asleep instead of concentrate! Ideally, your chair should be upright, with a straight back, and neither too hard nor too soft. It should support you comfortably, ensuring good posture.

Height of chair and desk

The chair should be high enough to allow your thighs to be parallel with the floor: this ensures that your sitting bones are taking the strain. On average, the desk should be approximately 20cm above the seat of the chair.

Distance of the eyes from the reading material

The natural distance for your eyes from your reading material is approximately 50cm. This makes it easier for your eyes to focus on groups of words (see page 46) and lessens the possibility of eye strain or headaches.

Your posture

Ideally your feet should be flat on the floor, your back upright, with the slight curve in your back maintained to give you support. If you sit up either too 'straight' or slumped, you will exhaust yourself and strain your back. Try either holding the book, or resting it on something so that it is slightly upright, rather than flat.

Sitting correctly has a number of benefits for the body:

⊙ Your brain receives the maximum flow of air and blood because your windpipe, veins and arteries are functioning unrestricted.

⊙ It will optimize the flow of energy up your spine and maximize the power of your brain.

⊙ If your body is alert then your brain knows something important is happening (conversely, if you sit in a slumped position, you are telling your brain that it is time to sleep!)

⊙ Your eyes can make full use of both your central and peripheral vision (see page 19).

...Then we'll begin
Watch the time

We all have peaks and troughs of concentration and each of us is likely to find that we read or concentrate best at different times of the day. There are 'larks' who work best between 5 and 9 in the morning; 'owls' who are at their most productive in the evening and at night; and others who find that late morning or early afternoon suits them best.

Many of us stick to a pattern of behaviour that we developed during our school or student days, so it is worth experimenting now to see whether a new pattern might work better for you.

Minimize interruptions

It is as important to minimize external interruptions and fidgeting when you are reading as it is to minimize the pauses while you read. External interruptions, such as telephone calls or personal diversions (i.e., unnecessary breaks or listening to the radio), are the enemy of concentration and focus.

Similarly, if you are worrying about something personal or are in physical discomfort, your preoccupation with other influences will reduce your concentration and comprehension.

The solution

Make your study environment sacrosanct and arrange it so that it is designed totally for the task. This means diverting your phone to voicemail if necessary, playing music that will help you concentrate and keeping your area free of distractions and temptations. (And turning your computer 'off', if you are not using it, so that you are not tempted onto the Internet.)

You will also work better if you are in good health, and regular aerobic exercise is an excellent way to keep your brain well oxygenated and your body strong and well supported.

Reading bites

⊙ Pay attention to your external environment: it is an important factor in your ability to perform to your optimum level.

⊙ Experiment with working at different times of day – see what works best for you.

⊙ Look after your inner self: maintain a calm, alert approach to your work and reading.

⊙ Treat your reading and work time as sacrosanct and avoid any unnecessary distractions.

Now that you are comfortable in your environment, in the next chapter I will introduce you to ways of expanding your vocabulary and with it the scope of your intellectual abilities.

7 MASTERMIND YOUR VOCABULARY

DID YOU KNOW THAT:

⊙ The average person's spoken vocabulary is about 1000 words.

⊙ The number of available words is over three million.

⊙ Improving your vocabulary raises your intelligence.

Vocabulary is important for many reasons. The person with a broad vocabulary is at a greater advantage in many situations:

⊙ in academic situations.

⊙ in business.

⊙ in social situations.

Most of us have more than one vocabulary; and usually we have at least three. These are:

⊙ the vocabulary we use in conversation.

⊙ the vocabulary we use when writing.

⊙ the vocabulary of word recognition.

Our conversational vocabulary tends to be limited to a maximum of 1000 words per person; our written vocabulary is greater because we take more care over our choice of words and sentence structure when we are drafting text; but the largest of the three is our recognition vocabulary. We understand many more words than we use.

In theory our conversational vocabulary should be as large as our recognition vocabulary, but that is rarely the case. It is possible, however, to increase the size of all three quite dramatically.

The development of vocabulary and sophisticated language structures is one of the defining characteristics of our evolutionary development and a skill that, if encouraged, provides extraordinary benefits. Speed reading isn't just about reading what others have written, it is also about developing a greater enjoyment and understanding of language in all its forms.

The next three sections are concerned with masterminding your vocabulary and will explore the word power of prefixes, suffixes and word roots. They are powerful shortcuts to increasing your language and vocabulary.

The power of prefixes

Prefixes are letters, syllables or words placed at the beginning of a word that alter meaning. Learning just a few prefixes will expand your vocabulary enormously. Many of them are concerned with position, opposition and movement. They are mini words with power.

In *The Speed Reading Book* you will find a comprehensive list of over 80 prefixes and their meanings. Of these, according to Joan Minninger PhD, just 14 are enough to provide keys to over 14,000 word meanings. The list of prefixes following is a selection of some of the most common ones; these were found within over 14,000 words from a standard desktop dictionary.

You will increase your potential vocabulary instantly by at least 10,000 words if you are able to remember and use these prefixes, by adding them to the beginning of words. Be on the lookout for them as you read from now on.

Words containing Key prefixes

Words	Prefix	Common meaning	Roots	Common meaning
precept	*pre-*	before	*capere*	take, seize
detain	*de-*	away, down	*tenere*	hold, have
intermittent	*inter-*	between, among	*mittere*	send
offer	*ob-*	against	*ferre*	bear, carry
insist	*in-*	into	*stare*	stand
monograph	*mono-*	alone, one	*graphein*	write
epilogue	*epi-*	upon	*logos*	speech, study of
advance	*ad-*	to, toward	*specere*	see
uncomplicated	*un-*	not together, with	*plicare*	fold
	com-			
non-extended	*non-*	out, beyond	*tender*	stretch
	ex-			
reproduction	*re-*	back, again	*ducere*	lead
	pro-	forward, for		
indisposed	*in-*	not	*ponere*	put, place
	dis-	apart, not		
over-sufficient	*over-*	above	*facere*	make, do
	sub-	under		
mistranscribe	*mis-*	wrong	*scribere*	write
	trans-	across, beyond		

Eye-Cue Vocabulary Exercise – Prefixes

Choose five words from the following list of six, to complete sentences 1–5 accurately:

Examinations   **Reviewing**   **Comprehension**

      Prepare   **Depress**   **Progress**

1 In order to be ready for a meeting or other event it is always best to .... in advance.

2 .... what you have learned will help to consolidate the associations in your memory.

3 Negative thoughts .... the brain and inhibit your ability to remember effectively.

4 Speed reading improves reading efficiency as well as ....

5 Preparing for .... needn't be daunting if you use speed reading and Mind Maps as your memory tools.

Now refer to page 90 for the answers

Fourteen suffixes

G = Greek, L = Latin, F = French, E = English

Suffix	Meaning	Example
-able, ible (L)	capable of, fit for	durable, comprehensible
-al, ail (L)	relating to quality	abdominal
-ance, ence, ant (L)	or action of forming	insurance, corpulence
	adjectives of quality, nouns signifying a personal agent or something producing an effect.	defiant, servant
-ation, -ition (L)	action or state of	condition, dilapidation
-er (E)	belonging to	farmer, New Yorker
-ism (E)	quality or doctrine of	realism, socialism
-ive (L)	nature of	creative, receptive
-ize, -ise (G)	make, practise, act like	modernize, advertise
-logy (G)	indicating a branch of knowledge	biology, psychology
-ly (E)	having the quality of	softly, quickly
-or (L)	a state or action, a person who, or thing which	victor, generator
-ous, -ose (L)	full of	murderous, anxious, officious, morose
-some	like	gladsome
-y (E)	condition	difficulty

The strength of suffixes

Suffixes are letters, syllables or words that are placed at the ends of words to alter meaning. They are often concerned with characteristics or qualities of something, or with changing from one part of speech to another (for example, from adjectives into verbs).

Eye-Cue Vocabulary Exercise – Suffixes

Choose five words from the following list of six, to complete sentences 1–5 accurately:

Minimal	Winsome	Psychology	Vociferous
	Hedonism	Practitioner	

1 A .... is one who works in a certain field, such as medicine.

2 The doctrine of pursuing pleasure as the highest good is known as ....

3 A charge for something which relates to the lowest or smallest price is ....

4 People who speak loudly and often are ....

5 The branch of knowledge that deals with the human mind and its functioning is known as ....

Now refer to page 90 for the answers.

Fourteen roots

Root	Meaning	Example
Aer	air	aerate, aeroplane
Am (from *amare*)	love	amorous, amateur, amiable
Chron	time	chronology, chronic
Dic, dict	say, speak	dictate
Equi	equal	equidistant
Graph	write	calligraphy, graphology, telegraph
Luc (from *lux*)	light	elucidate
pot, poss, poten (from *ponerte*)	be able	potential, possible
quaerere	ask, seek	question, inquiry, query
sent, sens (from *sentire*)	feel	sensitive, sentient
soph	wise	philosopher
spect (from *spicere*)	look	introspective, inspect
spir (from *spirare*)	breathe	inspiration
vid, vis (from *videre*)	see	supervisor, vision, provident

An A–Z of roots

This is the final section to focus on developing vocabulary and following is a list of 14 Latin and Greek root words that are commonly used in modern English.

Eye-Cue Vocabulary Exercise – Roots

Choose five words from the following list of six, to complete sentences 1–5 accurately:

Aerodynamics   **Equinox**   **Egocentric**

Querulous   **Chronometer**   **Amiable**

1 A person who is quarrelsome and discontented, and who complains in a questioning manner is ....

2 A person who is friendly and loveable is often described as ....

3 The .... is that time of year when both day and night are of equal length.

4 An instrument that finely measures time is a ....

5 The science which deals with the forces exerted by air and by gaseous fluids is ....

Now refer to page 90 for the answers.

How to use prefixes, suffixes and roots

The first time you look over these lists many of the words will seem unfamiliar, and getting to know the words may feel daunting. In order to make them more familiar and to help them become part of your daily vocabulary, I would like to offer the following tips:

● Browse through a good dictionary, and become familiar with the various ways in which these suffixes, prefixes and root words are used. Keep a record of Key Words and phrases that stand out for you and are useful in some way.

● Commit to making an effort to introduce one new word into your vocabulary each day. New words, like any information, need to be repeated a minimum of five times over an extended period before they will become a permanent feature of your memory.

● Listen for new and exciting words in conversation that you want to make a part of your growing vocabulary – and don't be shy about making a note of what you hear.

● Make a mental note to look up words that you don't understand when you read; but wait until you have finished reading the chapter, passage or paper. Don't interrupt the flow of what you are doing.

● Finally, you might be interested in tracking down a course that focuses on vocabulary training. Many of them are a helpful next step.

If you consciously improve your vocabulary by adding a few words and phrases each day, you will also improve your overall intellect as well as your general understanding and comprehension. At the same time your speed reading ability will accelerate because of your increased ability to spot Key Words and concepts and you will have few problems understanding what you are reading. In addition, you will no longer be tempted to back-skip as you read because you will have the confidence to know that your vocabulary is broad enough to support your general comprehension.

You now possess enough basic knowledge about your eyes, brain and about learning techniques to gain control over the ever-increasing flow of information that you encounter every day via emails, magazines, newspapers and television programmes.

You also have a vocabulary that will help you to enjoy any novel, poem, or other literature that you choose to enjoy. If you would now like to take your skills to the next level, you will find advanced speed reading techniques in my *Speed Reading Book* listed in the Further reading on page 95.

After a few days of focusing on improving your vocabulary levels, turn again to the reading speed and comprehension test on page 84 and you will see to what degree you have improved since you first began learning the techniques outlined in this book. Don't just stop there, though; choose to test yourself on an ongoing basis so that you are consciously improving your skills on an ongoing basis. There is also a progress chart included on page 87 where you can chart your results.

8 INCREASING THE PACE

By now you have gained an overview of the rudiments of speed reading and you will be ready to further increase your speed. The following links, tips and explanations for previewing books and other resources will enable you to 'up the pace' with ease. If you understand how information is organized and know where to look for answers you can increase the rate at which you devour knowledge.

The benefits of previewing

To preview something means just that: to pre-view, or to see before. If you allow your brain to *see* the whole text before speed reading it (by skimming, in association with one of the guided reading techniques) you will be able to navigate your way through it more effectively when you read it the second time. The purpose of previewing material before reading it is the same as the purpose of planning a route before driving from A to B. You need to know the terrain and decide whether to take the long scenic route or if a shortcut will suffice.

Previewing should be applied to everything you read, whether letters, reports, novels, articles – and *especially* emails. If done effectively it will save you an immense amount of time, and speed up your levels of reading and comprehension.

Strategies for effective previewing
Apply what you already know

Be aware of what you already know before you begin reading a book or a document and have an idea of what you want to achieve by reading it. Skim read the text first to discover the core elements. If the text is describing something you know already, make a note of the fact for future reference.

If you are required to read a revised version of an earlier document, use your honed speed reading techniques and your peripheral vision to go straight to the new material. You will recall many of the main points from the initial read-through. Take effective notes on everything you read so that you can refer back to them in future and use your previously acquired knowledge to assess the relevance of what you are reading. My Mind Map® technique is especially effective for this purpose. (There is a brief description of how to use it below, but for further information please refer to *Buzan Bites: Mind Mapping*, which is ideally laid out for the speed reader!)

How to take notes – using Mind Maps

The most effective speed reading skills in the world count for very little if the note-taking technique that goes with them is time-consuming and ineffective. The Mind Map® method of information storage and retrieval follows the same principles as speed reading and it has been designed to work in synergy with the brain, which means that your knowledge levels will increase the more you use them.

Your note-taking method should include:

⊙ Planning, focus and preview.

⊙ Clear recognition, assimilation and comprehension of facts.

⊙ A reflection of existing levels of knowledge.

⊙ A way of retaining information and ease of recall.

⊙ An easy form of communicating the information.

A Mind Map fulfils all these criteria.

In contrast, the disadvantages of 'normal' note-taking include:

⊙ A tendency to take indiscriminate notes without preview
– which means that the overall focus and intent are lost.

⊙ A preoccupation with 'getting everything down' on paper prevents ongoing critical analysis and appreciation of the subject matter.

⊙ Detailed note-taking bypasses the mind and distracts the listener who then misses what is really being said. (Just as it is possible to copy-type thousands of words of text without reading it.)

⊙ The volume of notes tends to become so great that the note-taker feels disinclined to refer back to them, or can make no sense of them, and has to begin again.

Effective note-taking is not about slavishly reproducing everything that has been said, but is a selective process. It should minimize the number of words written down and maximize the amount of information recalled.

The crucial element in effective note-taking is the selection of appropriate 'Key Words' and 'Images' that encapsulate the essence of everything you have read. A Key Word is both the word itself and a symbol of everything that relates to the word. A Key Image is much, much more than a picture. It is an image that is linked to and associated with a Key Word, and it will stimulate both sides of your brain and draw upon all your senses. When repeated, a Key Word or Key Image should trigger a recall not just of the basic concept, but of a whole wealth of information that goes with that concept.

Features of an effective Key Word:
- ⊙ Must trigger the right kind of memory.
- ⊙ Should not be too descriptive, abstract or general to be practical.
- ⊙ Must evoke a very specific image in your mind.
- ⊙ Must be personally satisfying.
- ⊙ Must have the ability to summarize information.

If you practise effective note-taking you will be amazed at how much more you can remember – and in how little space.

Mind Maps: the revolutionary note-taking technique

A Mind Map is a note-taking and brainstorming technique that has been created to work in tune with your brain by drawing on all your mental skills simultaneously. At one moment your brain uses all your associative and imaginative skills from your memory, while triggering connections between the right and left sides of your brain.

In Mind Map notes, instead of taking down whole sentences or making lists, a combination of Key Words and Key Images is used to capture the essence of the information and to act as precise memory triggers to recall the information.

As you build up your Mind Map, so your brain creates an integrated map of the whole of the territory you are recording. A Mind Map therefore becomes a multi-dimensional note from your own brain that reproduces all you want to remember in a unique fashion. It is a powerful graphic technique that harnesses the power of your brain to the full and unlocks your true potential. Mind Maps work *with* your memory, to make it easy for you to recall information on demand.

I first devised the Mind Map concept over 35 years ago in order to help me make sense of the wealth of material that I had to read and absorb as a student. The technique enabled me to achieve excellent results, and it has been adopted by hundreds of millions of people around the world since then, from all walks of life. From teaching to training to brainstorming; in education, business, politics and in the home; Mind Maps are helping people to capture complex information simply, and to generate new ideas in a limitless fashion.

Mind Maps can be used in partnership with your speed reading skills to record every aspect of your reading, studying and learning, and will enhance all aspects of your performance.

(More information about the practice and principles of Mind Map creation and memory recall can be found in two further titles in this series: *Buzan Bites: Mind Mapping* and *Buzan Bites: Brilliant Memory*.)

9 TEST YOUR PROGRESS

You are nearing the end of this introduction to speed reading. The next stage will be for you to continue practising with the new skills you have learned and, if you wish to develop your speed-reading abilities further, to take the course in *The Speed Reading Book*.

As you have learned the speed reading techniques set out in this *Bite* you will have been practising your reading speeds and developing your ability to assimilate and comprehend information. Now, through the following passage – The Intelligence War – you will be able to test both your reading speed and comprehension, and measure how far you have progressed.

When you are ready to take the test, make sure you have your watch by your side, and do your reading privately (someone timing you or watching you inevitably interferes with your comprehension and tends to make some people read more hurriedly than usual, others more slowly).

When you have reached the end of the article, immediately check your watch and calculate your speed. Full instructions will be given on how to do this.

Your comprehension will be tested at the end with 15 multiple-choice and true/false questions.

Self Test: The Intelligence War – at the Front with Brain Training
New World Trends

Stock market analysts watch, like hawks, ten individuals in Silicon Valley. When there is even a hint that one might move from Company A to Company B, the world's stock markets shift.

The English Manpower Services Commission recently published a survey in which it was noted that, of the top ten per cent of British companies, 80 per cent invested considerable money and time in training; and in the bottom ten per cent of companies no money or time was invested.

In Minnesota, the Plato Computer Education Project has already raised the thinking and academic performance levels of 200,000 pupils.

In the armed forces of an increasing number of countries, mental martial arts are becoming as important as physical combat skills.

National Olympic squads are devoting as much as 40 per cent of their training time to the development of positive mind set, mental stamina and visualization.

In the Fortune 500 (the 500 top-earning US companies), the top five computer companies alone have spent over a billion dollars on educating their employees, and the development of intellectual capital has become the main priority, including the development of the world's most powerful currency – the currency of intelligence.

In Caracas, Dr Luis Alberto Machado became the first person to be given a government portfolio as Minister of Intelligence, with a political mandate to increase the mental power of the nation.

We are witnessing a quantum leap in human evolution – the awareness by intelligence of itself, and the concomitant awareness that this intelligence can be nurtured to astounding advantage.

This encouraging news must be considered in the context of the most significant problem areas as defined by the business community.

Over the last 20 years over 100,000 people from each of the five major continents have been polled. The top 20 areas commonly mentioned as requiring improvement are:

1   Reading speed
2   Reading comprehension
3   General study skills
4   Handling the information explosion
5   Memory
6   Concentration
7   Oral communication skills
8   Written communication skills
9   Creative thinking
10 Planning
11 Note-taking
12 Problem analysis
13 Problem solving
14 Motivation
15 Analytical thinking
16 Examination techniques
17 Prioritizing
18 Time management
19 Assimilation of information
20 Getting started (procrastination)
21 Mental ability declining with age

With the aid of modern research on the functioning of the brain, each of these problems can be tackled with relative ease. This research covers:

1 The functions of the left and right cortex
2 Mind Mapping
3 Super-speed and range reading/intellectual commando units
4 Mnemonic techniques
5 Memory loss after learning
6 The brain cell
7 Mental abilities and ageing

The functions of the left and right cortex

It has now become common knowledge that the left and right
cortical structures of the brain tend to deal with different
intellectual functions. The left cortex primarily handles logic,
words, numbers, sequence, analysis, linearity and listing, while
the right cortex processes rhythm, colour, imagination, daydreaming, spatial relationships and dimension.

What has recently been realized is that the left cortex is not
the 'academic' side, nor is the right cortex the 'creative, intuitive,
emotional' side. We now know from volumes of research that
both sides need to be used in conjunction with each other for
there to be both academic and creative success.

The Einsteins, Newtons, Cézannes and Mozarts of this
world, like the great business geniuses, combined their
linguistic, numerical and analytical skills with imagination and
visualization in order to produce their creative masterpieces.

Mind Maps

Using this basic knowledge of our mental functioning, it is
possible to train people in order to solve each of these problem
areas, often producing incremental improvements of 500 per cent.

One of the modern methods of achieving such
improvements is Mind Mapping.

In traditional note-taking, whether it be for remembering information, for preparing written or oral communication, for organizing your thoughts, for problem analysis, for planning or for creative thinking, the standard mode of presentation is linear: either sentences, short lists of phrases, or numerically and alphabetically ordered lists. These methods, because of their lack of colour, visual rhythm, image and spatial relationships, cauterize the brain's thinking capacities, and literally impede each of the aforementioned mental processes.

Mind Mapping, by contrast, uses the full range of the brain's abilities, placing an image in the centre of the page in order to facilitate memorization and the creative generation of ideas, and subsequently branching out in associative networks that mirror externally the brain's internal structures. Using this approach, you can prepare speeches in minutes rather than days; problems can be solved both more comprehensively and more rapidly; memory can be improved from absent to perfect; and creative thinkers can generate a limitless number of ideas rather than a truncated list.

Super-speed and range reading/intellectual commando units

By combining Mind Mapping with new super-speed and range reading techniques (which allow speeds of well over 1000 words per minute along with excellent comprehension, and eventual effective reading speeds of about 10,000 words per minute), one can form intellectual commando units.

Reading at these advanced speeds, Mind Mapping in detail the outline of the book and its chapters, and exchanging the information gathered by using advanced Mind Mapping and presentation skills, it is possible for four or more individuals to acquire, integrate, memorize and begin to apply in their professional situation four complete books' worth of new information in one day.

These techniques have recently been applied in the multinational organizations Nabisco and Digital Computers. In these instances, 40 and 120 senior executives respectively divided their groups into four. Each individual in each of the four sub-groups spent two hours applying speed and range reading techniques to one of the four selected books.

When the two hours were completed, the members of each sub-group discussed among themselves their understandings, interpretations and reactions to the book. Each sub-group then chose one representative who gave a comprehensive lecture to all the members of the three other sub-groups. This process was repeated four times, and at the end of each day, 40 and 120 senior executives in each company walked out of their seminar room with four complete new books' worth of information not only in their heads, but integrated, analyzed and memorized.

This approach can be similarly used in the family situation, and is already being used in families around the world.

Recently, a Mexican family applied it to their three children, ranging in age from 6 to 15. Within two months, each child was the top student in its year, having been able to complete in two days, with the help of the other family members, what the average child/student completes in a year.

Mnemonic techniques

Mnemonic techniques were originally invented by the Greeks, and were thought to be 'tricks'. We now realize that these devices are soundly based on the brain's functioning, and that, when applied appropriately, they can dramatically improve anyone's memory.

Mnemonic techniques require you to use the principles of association and imagination, to create dramatic, colourful, sensual and consequently unforgettable images in your mind.

The Mind Map is in fact a multi-dimensional mnemonic, using the brain's inbuilt functions to imprint more effectively data/information upon itself.

Using mnemonics, businessmen have been trained to remember perfectly 40 newly introduced people, and to similarly memorize lists of over 100 products, with relevant facts and data. These techniques are now being applied at the IBM Training Centre in Stockholm, and have had a major impact on the success of their 17-week introductory training programme. The same techniques have been used in the World Memory Championships.

There is an increasing awareness that learning how to learn before any other training has been given is good business sense. This is why a number of the more progressive international organizations are now making mnemonics the obligatory 'front end' to all their training courses. Simple calculation shows that, if £1,000,000 is spent on training, and 80 per cent of that training is forgotten within two weeks, £800,000 has been lost during that same period!

Memory loss after learning

Memory loss after learning is dramatic.

After a one-hour learning period, there is a short rise in the recall of information as the brain integrates the new data. This is followed by a dramatic decline in which, after 24 hours, as much as 80 per cent of detail is lost.

The scale remains roughly the same regardless of the length of input time. Thus a three-day course is more or less forgotten within one to two weeks of completion.

The implications are disturbing; if a multinational firm spends $50 million per year on training and there is no appropriate reviewing programmed into the educational structure, $40 million will have been lost with incredible efficiency within a few days of that training's completion.

By gaining a simple understanding of the memory's rhythms, it is possible not only to avert this decline, but also to train people in such a way as to increase the amount learned and retained.

The brain cell

In recent years the brain cell has become the new frontier in the human search for knowledge.

Not only do we each have 1,000,000,000,000 brain cells, but the interconnections between them can form a staggeringly large number of patterns and permutations. This number, calculated by the Russian neuro-anatomist Pyotr K. Anokhin, is one followed by ten million kilometres of standard typewritten noughts!

With our inherent capacity to integrate and juggle multiple billions of bits of data, it has become apparent to those involved in brain research that adequate training of our phenomenal biocomputer (which can calculate in one second what it would take the Cray computer, at 400 million calculations per second, 100 years to accomplish) will enormously accelerate and increase our ability to problem solve, to analyze, to prioritize, to create and to communicate.

Mental abilities and ageing

'They die!' is the usual chorus from people in response to the question: 'What happens to your brain cells as they get older?' It is usually voiced with extraordinary and surprising enthusiasm.

However, one of the most delightful pieces of news from modern brain research comes from Dr Marion Diamond of the

University of California, who has recently confirmed that there is no evidence of brain cell loss with age in normal, active and healthy brains.

On the contrary, research is now indicating that, if the brain is used and trained, there is a biological increase in its interconnective complexity, i.e. the person's intelligence is raised.

Training of people in their sixties, seventies, eighties and nineties has shown that, in every area of mental performance, statistically significant and permanent improvements can be made.

We are at the beginning of an unprecedented revolution: the quantum leap in the development of human intelligence.

On the personal front, in education and in business, information from psychological, neuro-physiological and educational laboratories is being used to solve problems that were hitherto accepted as an inevitable part of the ageing process.

By applying our knowledge of the brain's separate functions, by externally reflecting our internal processes in Mind Map form, by making use of the innate elements and rhythms of memory, and by applying our knowledge of the brain cell and the possibilities for continued mental improvement throughout life, we realize that the intelligence war can indeed be won.

Stop Your Timer Now
Length of time: .... mins

Next, calculate your reading speed in words per minute (wpm) by simply dividing the number of words in the passage (in this case 1871) by the time (in minutes) you took.

Speed Reading Formula:
$$\text{words per minute (wpm)} = \frac{\text{number of words}}{\text{time}}$$

When you have completed your calculation, enter the number in the wpm slot at the end of this paragraph, and enter it on your Progress Chart and your Progress Graph on pages 87 and 88.

Words per minute:

Self Test: Comprehension

For each question, either circle 'True' or 'False' or tick the right answer.

1 The top 80 per cent of British companies invest considerable money and time in training.   True/False

2 National Olympic squads are devoting as much as:
(a) 20 per cent
(b) 30 per cent
(c) 40 per cent
(d) 50 per cent
of their training time to the development of positive mind set, mental stamina and visualization.

3 The first person to be given a government portfolio as Minister of Intelligence was:
(a) Dr Marion Diamond
(b) Dr Luis Alberto Machado
(c) Dominic O'Brien
(d) Plato

4 Number is mainly a left-cortex function.   True/False

5 The Einsteins, Newtons, Cézannes and Mozarts of this world were successful because they primarily combined:
(a) number with logic
(b) words with analysis
(c) colour with rhythm
(d) analysis with imagination

6 In Mind Mapping, you:
(a) place an image in the centre
(b) place a word in the centre
(c) place nothing in the centre
(d) always place a word and an image in the centre

7 Using new super-speed and range reading techniques, you should be able to establish new normal speeds of well over:
(a) 500 words per minute
(b) 1000 words per minute
(c) 10,000 words per minute
(d) 100,000 words per minute

8 The two companies who formed intellectual commando units for studying books were:
(a) IBM and Coca-Cola
(b) Digital and Nabisco
(c) Nabisco and Microsoft
(d) IBM and ICL

9 Mnemonic techniques were originally invented by:
(a) the Chinese
(b) the Romans
(c) the Greeks
(d) Plato

10 After a one-hour period there is:
(a) a short rise in the recall of information
(b) a levelling off in the recall of information
(c) a short drop in the recall of information
(d) a rapid drop in the recall of information

11 Twenty-four hours after a learning period the following percentage of detail is often lost:
(a) 60 per cent
(b) 70 per cent
(c) 80 per cent
(d) 90 per cent

12 The number of brain cells in the average brain is:
(a) a million
(b) a thousand million
(c) a million million
(d) a thousand million million

13 The Cray computer is finally approaching the capacity of the brain in its overall ability to calculate.   True/False

14 Dr Marion Diamond recently confirmed that there is:
(a) no evidence of brain cell loss with age in normal active and healthy brains
(b) no evidence of brain cell loss with age in any brain
(c) no evidence of brain cell loss with age in brains under 40
(d) evidence of slight brain cell loss with age in normal active and healthy brains

15 With adequate training, statistically significant and permanent improvements in intelligence can be made in people up to the age of:
(a) 60
(b) 70
(c) 80
(d) 90

Check your answers against those on page 90. Then divide your score by 15 and multiply by 100 to calculate your percentage comprehension.

Comprehension score: ..... out of 15

.......per cent

Now enter your score in your Progress Chart and your Progress Graph.

Progress chart

Ideally use one colour for recording your speed and another colour for your comprehension.

Reading number	Time (minute-second)	Speed (wpm)	Comprehension
2			
3			
4			
5			
6			
7			
8			
9			
10			

Progress graph

speed 'wpm'	1	2	3	4	5	6	7	8	9
1000									
900									
800									
700									
600									
500									
400									
300									
200									
100									
0									

progress
over time

| 10 | 11 | 12 | 13 | 14 | 15 | 16 | 17 | 18 |

Answers

Page 59: Eye-Cue Vocabulary Exercise – Prefixes
1: prepare; 2: reviewing; 3: depress; 4: comprehension;
5: examinations

Page 61: Eye-Cue Vocabulary Exercise – Suffixes
1: practitioner; 2: hedonism; 3: minimal; 4: vociferous;
5: psychology

Page 63: Eye-Cue Vocabulary Exercise – Roots
1: quarulous; 2: amiable; 3: equinox; 4: chronometer;
5: aerodynamics

Page 84: Self Test: Comprehension
1 False; 2 (c) 40 per cent; 3 (b) Dr Machado; 4 True;
5 (d) analysis with imagination; 6 (a) place an image in the
centre; 7 (b) 1000 wpm; 8 Digital and Nabisco; 9 (c) The Greeks;
10 (c) a short rise; 11 (c) 80 per cent; 12 (c) a million million;
13 False; 14 (a) no evidence of brain cell loss with age in normal
active and healthy brains; 15 (d) 90

Conclusion

You have now entered the growing international community of Speed Readers – congratulations!

Your new knowledge of the expanded definition of reading will enable you to embrace the written word in a much more rounded way, with greater confidence and success.

By applying your new knowledge of what *really* happens when the extraordinary team of your eyes and your brain work together, you will no longer be burdened by what many people have defined as reading problems; **you** now know that they are 'friends in disguise', and can be turned with a 'flick-of-the-brain' into major reading skills.

In addition, your reading skills are newly enhanced by the building blocks of vocabulary. These are like Lego pieces. They will allow you to construct thousands of new 'buildings of meaning'. These in turn will expand your comprehension and understanding, and because of this will allow you to read more freely and smoothly at more rapid and elegant speeds.

Combining your increased vocabulary with the meta-knowledge management tool – the Mind Map – your ability to note, remember and create from what you have read will now be under your control, and will be infinite.

Contained within the speed reading formulas you have been given are the techniques for continuing your speed reading progress. Make sure you develop a plan for your own continued reading programme, and within that incorporate continuing to find out more about the field you have just entered. If you do so, your speeds will continue to increase, your comprehension to improve and your internal database to grow exponentially.

Remember today and for the rest of your life, that your eyes truly **are** amazing. Bring to mind, before any serious reading, the fact that you have *two hundred and sixty million* (260,000,000) light receivers, which are connected to a brain of universally immense capacity. Reading, for such a super-system, should be both a pleasure and a delight, as for you it will be.

Remember also that it is your Mind's Eye that is the master in all this, and that by using skimming and scanning, and the multiple guiding techniques, you will allow that master to be more masterful still.

At the end of the Twentieth Century many education systems, businesses, and governments declared that we were entering the Knowledge Age.

With the incredible acceleration of both information and our knowledge about the extraordinary capacity of the human brain, they are already out-of-date.

At the beginning of the Twenty-first Century, what we are entering is the age of Intellectual Capital. In this age, Learning How to Learn will be the crucial and paramount skill.

We are entering a period in the history of human development where the ability to recognize and assimilate information at speed, to comprehend and link it to existing brain databases of previous knowledge, to then store it effectively and to recall it instantaneously and upon demand and to then combine all of these elements with the ability to create and communicate from the basis of what has been learned, will be the skills that will define success in the future.

You are now fully equipped for that future.